Exploring the Galaxy

Saturn

by Thomas K. Adamson

Consulting Editor: Gail Saunders-Smith, Ph.D.

Consultant: James Gerard
Aerospace Education Specialist, NASA
Kennedy Space Center, Florida

Capstone
press

Mankato, Minnesota

Pebble Plus is published by Capstone Press
151 Good Counsel Drive, P.O. Box 669, Mankato, Minnesota 56002
http://www.capstone-press.com

1 2 3 4 5 6 08 07 06 05 04 03

Library of Congress Cataloging-in-Publication Data
Adamson, Thomas K., 1970–
    Saturn / by Thomas K. Adamson.
    p. cm.—(Pebble Plus: exploring the galaxy)
    Summary: Simple text and photographs describe the planet Saturn.
    Includes bibliographical references and index.
    ISBN 0-7368-2117-1 (hardcover)
    1. Saturn (Planet)—Juvenile literature. [1. Saturn (Planet)] I. Title. II. Series.
QB671 .A32 2004
523.46—dc21   2002155596

Editorial Credits
Mari C. Schuh, editor; Kia Adams, designer; Alta Schaffer, photo researcher; Eric Kudalis, product planning editor

Photo Credits
Digital Vision, 5 (Venus), 8–9, 10–11
PhotoDisc Inc., cover, 4 (Neptune); 5 (Mars, Mercury, Sun, Saturn, Earth), 17 (both); Stock Trek, 1, 12–13, 14–15; PhotoDisc Imaging, 7
Photo Researchers Inc./Jerry Lodriguss, 21
NASA, 4 (Pluto), 5 (Jupiter); JPL/Caltech, 5 (Uranus); Photri-Microstock, 19

Note: Some of the images in this book are false-color images that use artificial colors to enhance planet features.

Note to Parents and Teachers

The Exploring the Galaxy series supports national science standards related to earth science. This book describes and illustrates the planet Saturn. The photographs support early readers in understanding the text. The repetition of words and phrases helps early readers learn new words. This book also introduces early readers to subject-specific vocabulary words, which are defined in the Glossary section. Early readers may need assistance to read some words and to use the Table of Contents, Glossary, Read More, Internet Sites, and Index/Word List sections of the book.

Word Count: 138
Early-Intervention Level: 14

Table of Contents

Saturn

Saturn is the sixth planet
from the Sun. Saturn is
the second largest planet
in the solar system.

The Solar System

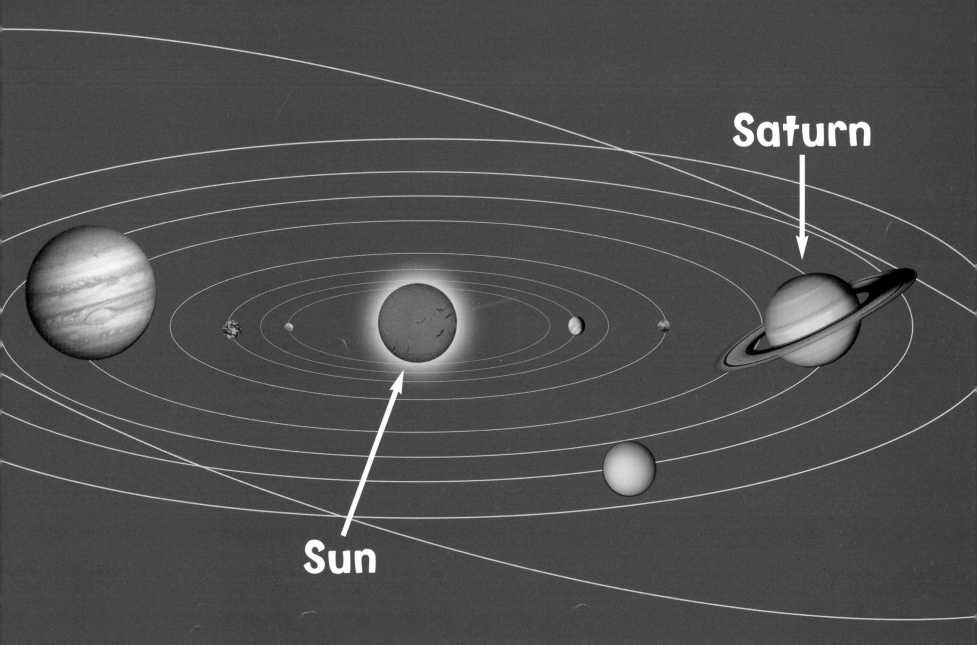

Saturn

Sun

Saturn is a ball of gases and clouds. Saturn is called a gas giant.

Thick clouds cover Saturn.
Saturn does not have a solid
surface. A spacecraft cannot
land on Saturn.

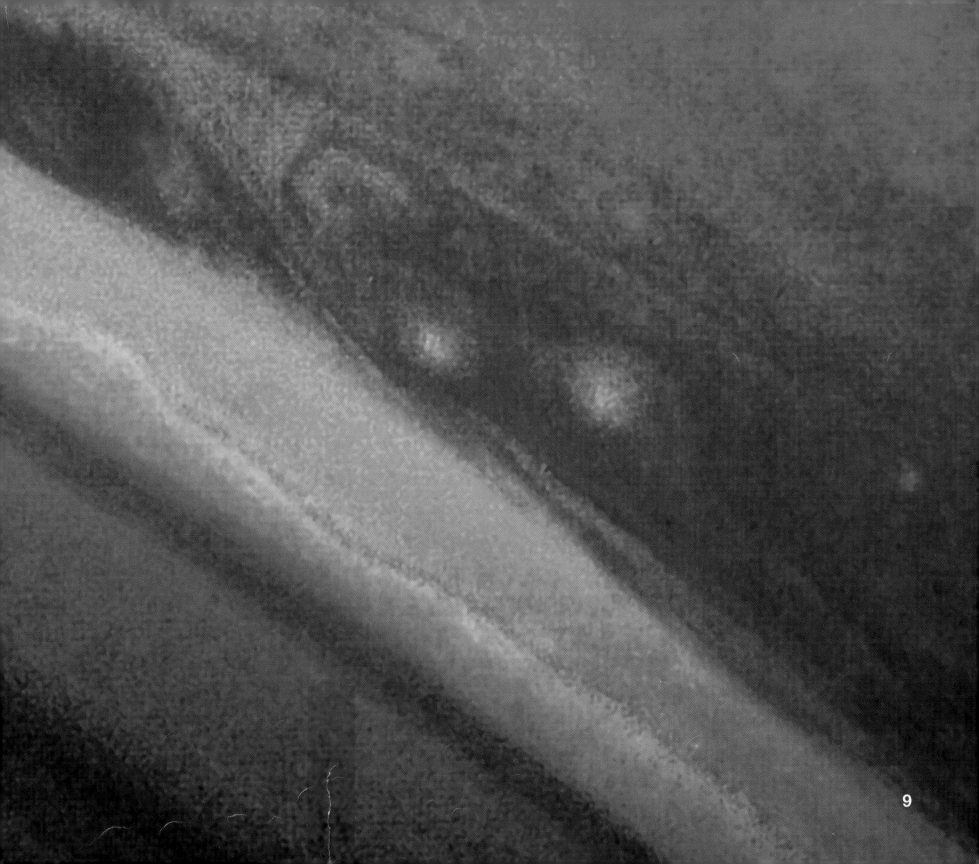

At least 31 moons move around Saturn. Earth has only one moon.

Saturn's Rings

Saturn's rings are wide and flat. People on Earth can see the rings with a telescope.

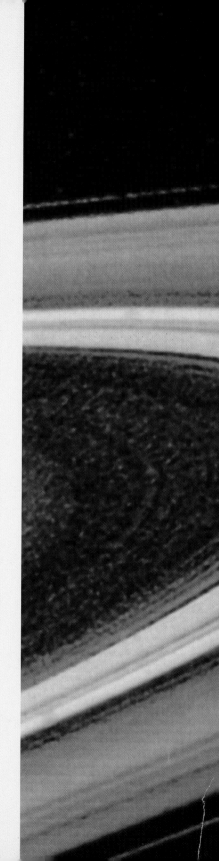

Saturn's rings are pieces of rock and ice. Some pieces are as big as a car.

Saturn's Size

Saturn and its rings
are almost 10 times
wider than Earth.

Earth

Saturn

People and Saturn

It is too cold for people to live on Saturn. The air is so cold on Saturn that people cannot breathe.

People can see Saturn
from Earth. Saturn looks
like a bright star.

Saturn

Glossary

gas—a substance, such as air, that spreads to fill any space that holds it; Saturn is mostly made of gases.

moon—an object that moves around a planet

planet—a large object that moves around the Sun; Saturn is the sixth planet from the Sun.

solar system—the Sun and the objects that move around it; our solar system has nine planets and many moons, asteroids, and comets.

spacecraft—a vehicle used to travel in space

star—a large ball of burning gases in space; the Sun is a star.

Sun—the star that the planets move around; the Sun provides light and heat to the planets.

surface—the outside or outermost area of something

telescope—a tool people use to look at planets and other objects in space

Read More

Goss, Tim. *Saturn.* The Universe. Chicago: Heinemann Library, 2002.

Rau, Dana Meachen. *Saturn.* Our Solar System. Minneapolis: Compass Point Books, 2003.

Vogt, Gregory. *Saturn.* The Galaxy. Mankato, Minn.: Bridgestone Books, 2000.

Internet Sites

Do you want to find out more about Saturn and the solar system? Let FactHound, our fact-finding hound dog, do the research for you.

Here's how:

1) Visit *http://www.facthound.com*

2) Type in the **Book ID** number: **0736821171**

3) Click on **FETCH IT**.

FactHound will fetch Internet sites picked by our editors just for you!

Index/Word List